BATTLES &

BOARDS

Silas Carter's Quest for the Artificial Floor

PHILL AKINWALE, OPM3, PMP

Real World Project Management Training Solutions

Battles and Boards
Published by Praizion Media
P.O Box 22241, Mesa, AZ 85277
E-mail: info@praizion.com
www.praizion.com

Author
Phillip Akirwale, MSc, OPM3, PMP, PMI-ACP, CAPM, PSM, CSM

ISBN 978-1-934579-52-7

9 781934 579527

This work of fiction is inspired by themes of corporate warfare, technological innovation, and personal ambition. While the story may draw on certain real-world concepts, technologies, and business practices, the characters, events, companies, and any resemblance to actual persons, living or dead, or to actual events or locales, are entirely coincidental. The views and opinions expressed within this work are solely those of the characters and do not necessarily reflect the views, opinions, or practices of any actual individuals, companies, industries, or regulatory bodies.

The author and publisher have made every effort to ensure the accuracy of the information within the story, particularly as it pertains to technological aspects and business practices. However, due to the fictional nature of the work, readers should not rely on the content as a basis for real-world decision-making or as a precise representation of current or future technological advancements.

CONTENTS

Silas Carter's office had never looked so dim. Despite the early morning sunlight filtering through the blinds, the room felt cloaked in a shadow of despair. The once vibrant heart of OakLine, the Midwest's most innovative flooring firm, now pulsated with anxiety and uncertainty.

Silas, a middle-aged man with sharp features and a countenance that once exuded confidence, stared at the financial reports on his desk. The numbers were clear, and they were ruthless. The firm was down to its last million dollars, and with salaries at $800K monthly, the end was near.

He glanced at the framed pictures on the wall, images of

OakLine's golden years, when innovation was their watchword, and success seemed inevitable. Now, it all seemed like a distant dream.

"Silas?" The soft voice of Mary, his ever-loyal admin, broke the silence. "Jackson is here to see you."

Silas looked up and managed a weak smile. "Send him in, Mary."

Jackson Evans, the Chairman of the Board, entered the room, his face lined with concern. A tall man in his sixties, Jackson had been with OakLine since its inception. His wisdom and guidance had steered the company through many storms, but this one seemed insurmountable.

"Silas, we need to talk," Jackson said, his voice weighed down by the gravity of their situation.

"I know, Jackson," Silas replied, his voice barely above a whisper. "I've been trying to find a way out, but everything seems to be closing in on us."

Jackson took a seat and placed a hand on Silas's shoulder. "I believe in you, Silas. I always have. But we need to face the reality. CedarCorp's offer to acquire us might be our only option."

Silas's eyes widened, his body stiffening. CedarCorp's offer had been an insult, a slap in the face. They were looking to buy OakLine for pennies on the dollar, and the mere mention of it felt like a betrayal.

"We can't give in to them, Jackson," Silas protested. "CedarCorp has been our rival for years. We can't just hand them our legacy."

"I understand, Silas, but we have to think about our employees, our families, our responsibilities," Jackson reasoned, his eyes filled with compassion.

Silas's heart ached. He knew that Jackson was right, but the thought of giving up, of surrendering to Graham, CedarCorp's cunning and manipulative executive, was unbearable.

"We still have time," Silas insisted, his voice filled with determination. "I won't let OakLine die. Not like this."

Jackson sighed, recognizing the fire in Silas's eyes. "Alright, Silas. I'll stand by you. But we need a plan, and we need it fast."

As Jackson left the room, Silas's mind raced. He knew that the odds were against him, that failure was looming, but he couldn't give up. OakLine was his life's work, his passion, his identity.

He looked out the window, watching the city's hustle and bustle, feeling a strange connection with the chaos outside. In the midst of the turmoil, there had to be a way, a path to redemption.

The phone on his desk rang, jolting him from his thoughts. He picked it up, his heart pounding.

"Silas, it's Graham from CedarCorp," the voice on the other end oozed with smug satisfaction. "I heard you're considering our offer. Wise choice."

Silas's blood boiled. Graham's arrogance was insufferable, his intentions clear. He wanted to see OakLine crumble, to dance on its grave.

"We haven't made any decisions yet, Graham," Silas replied, his voice icy.

"Oh, come now, Silas," Graham taunted. "We both know that OakLine is on its last legs. Accept our offer, and at least you'll walk away with something."

Silas's grip on the phone tightened. He wanted to lash out, to tell Graham exactly what he thought of him and his offer, but he knew he had to be careful.

"We'll see, Graham," Silas said, his voice controlled. "We'll see."

As he hung up, Silas's mind whirred into action. He knew that he had to find a way to save OakLine, to prove Graham wrong, to reclaim his legacy.

The battle had just begun, and Silas was ready to fight.

Chapter 2: A Glimmer of Hope

Silas's sleep was restless that night, haunted by the specter of CedarCorp's offer and the imminent collapse of OakLine. The once proud and innovative flooring firm seemed to be disintegrating before his very eyes.

The next morning, Silas arrived at the office early, his mind still churning with thoughts of desperation and defeat. The corridors of OakLine, once bustling with creativity and enthusiasm, now felt like a mausoleum, echoing with the ghosts of better days.

Mary, always the early bird, greeted him with a warm smile and a steaming cup of coffee. Her unwavering support was a beacon of comfort in these dark times.

"Morning, Silas," she said, her eyes revealing a mix of concern and optimism. "How are you holding up?"

Silas managed a weak smile, accepting the coffee. "Surviving, Mary. Just surviving."

Mary's eyes twinkled with a knowing look. "You'll pull us through, Silas. I know you will."

Silas's heart ached with gratitude for her faith in him, but he couldn't shake the feeling of dread that seemed to cling to him like a shadow.

As he settled into his office, Silas's eyes were drawn to the innovative flooring designs that once made OakLine a household name. The memories of those glory days were both inspiring and painful, a reminder of what once was and what might never be again.

But amidst the despair, a spark of curiosity ignited within him. What if there was a way to breathe new life into OakLine? What if innovation, the very thing that had once propelled them to greatness, could save them now?

The answer came in the form of a magazine article that caught his eye. A piece on Artificial Intelligence and its potential applications in the manufacturing industry. The idea was tantalizing, a fusion of technology and creativity that could revolutionize OakLine's approach to flooring design.

He read the article again and again, his mind racing with

possibilities. The concept was bold, untested in their industry, but it held promise. A promise of something new, something groundbreaking.

His excitement growing, Silas picked up the phone and dialed a number he found at the end of the article. Dr. Elaine Thompson, an eccentric AI expert with a reputation for thinking outside the box.

"Dr. Thompson?" Silas's voice was charged with anticipation. "My name is Silas Carter, CEO of OakLine. I just read your article, and I think you might be the key to saving my company."

There was a pause, then a soft chuckle on the other end. "Well, Mr. Carter, I do love a challenge. Tell me more."

Silas's heart soared as he explained his vision, his idea of merging AI with flooring design to create something unique. Dr. Thompson listened intently, her interest piqued.

"I'll be honest, Mr. Carter," she finally said, her voice filled with intrigue. "This is uncharted territory, but I think we can make it work. Let's meet and explore the possibilities."

Silas hung up the phone, a newfound hope swelling within him. The path ahead was uncertain, fraught with risk, but he felt alive, invigorated by the prospect of innovation once more.

He looked out the window, his eyes fixed on the horizon. The future was still uncertain, but for the first time in a long time, he could see a glimmer of hope.

As he turned back to his desk, determination etched on his face, Silas knew that he had taken the first step on a journey that could either save OakLine or seal its fate.

But one thing was certain; he wouldn't go down without a fight.

Chapter 3: The Race Against Time

The conference room at OakLine had seen its fair share of meetings, but none quite like this. Silas, Dr. Elaine Thompson, Mary, and a few key team members gathered around a table littered with blueprints, laptops, and more coffee cups than any health professional would deem advisable.

Dr. Elaine was a striking figure, her wild curls tamed by vibrant scarves, her eyes sparkling with intelligence and mischief. She had a way of making complex AI concepts sound like casual dinner conversation, and her wit was as sharp as her mind.

"So, what you're telling me, Silas," she said, leaning back in her chair and eyeing him with an impish grin, "is that you want to make floors intelligent?"

Silas chuckled, caught off guard by her humor. "Not exactly intelligent, Dr. Thompson. Just more innovative and efficient."

"Ah, so no dancing floors then?" she quipped, her eyes twinkling. "Pity, I was looking forward to a waltz."

The room erupted in laughter, the tension momentarily broken. It was a welcome reprieve from the weight of their situation.

Once the laughter subsided, they dove into the details. The idea was to use AI algorithms to optimize production, create new designs, and reduce waste. It was ambitious, it was untested, but it was their best shot.

As the days turned into weeks, the team worked tirelessly, fueled by a shared vision and copious amounts of caffeine. Dr. Elaine's eccentricities were a constant source of amusement and inspiration.

"Mary, darling, would you pass the quantum entanglement theory?" she'd ask, referring to the sugar bowl.

Or during a particularly challenging coding session: "I do believe this algorithm needs a bit more spice, perhaps a dash of chaos theory?"

Her humor kept them going, even when the odds seemed insurmountable.

But it wasn't all fun and games. Graham, CedarCorp's cunning executive, had caught wind of their project and was determined to sabotage their efforts. He hired a tech-savvy spy to infiltrate OakLine's system, hoping to steal their research or, at the very least, slow them down.

Silas knew they were being watched. He could feel Graham's presence, like a snake in the grass, waiting to strike. But he wouldn't be deterred. The stakes were too high, the opportunity too great.

As the weeks turned into months, their hard work began to pay off. The AI-driven solution was taking shape, the algorithms fine-tuned, the designs innovative and fresh.

Silas could see the future of OakLine, a future filled with promise and success. He could see the smiles on the faces of his employees, the pride in their work, the resurgence of the company he loved.

But time was running out. The money was dwindling, and Graham's shadow was growing ever closer.

In a moment of quiet reflection, Silas found himself in his office, looking at the old pictures on the wall. He remembered the joy of those early days, the thrill of innovation, the satisfaction of success.

He knew that he was on the brink of something extraordinary, something that could change the face of the flooring industry. But he also knew that the race against time was far from over.

With a determined smile, he turned back to his work, ready to face the challenges ahead.

For OakLine, for his team, for himself, Silas Carter was ready to win.

Chapter 4: Betrayal and Redemption

The air was thick with tension as Silas stood before his team, his face pale, his eyes filled with disbelief. A breach in their security system had been discovered, and it was clear that someone within OakLine had been feeding information to CedarCorp.

The room was silent, each person grappling with the weight of the revelation. The tight-knit team, bound by a shared vision and relentless pursuit of innovation, had been infiltrated by betrayal.

"Who?" Silas finally asked, his voice breaking. "Who would do this to us?"

No one spoke. Accusations hung in the air, unspoken but palpable.

Days turned into a frantic search for the mole, a search that was as painful as it was necessary. Trust, once the bedrock of OakLine's culture, had been shattered, replaced by suspicion and doubt.

The culprit was eventually found. Lenny, a young and overlooked programmer, had been seduced by Graham's promises of wealth and success. His guilt was evident, his remorse genuine, but the damage was done.

Silas's heart ached as he confronted Lenny, the young man's eyes filled with shame and fear.

"Why, Lenny?" Silas asked, his voice filled with sorrow rather than anger. "Why did you betray us?"

Lenny's voice trembled as he spoke, his words a mix of regret and desperation. "I was scared, Mr. Carter. Scared of losing my job, my future. Graham promised me security, success. I didn't think... I didn't realize what I was doing."

Silas looked into Lenny's eyes, seeing the young man's torment, his struggle with guilt. He saw a reflection of his own fear, his own uncertainty.

In that moment, Silas realized that Lenny's betrayal was not born of malice but of fear. A fear that had been expertly manipulated by Graham, a fear that spoke to the very core of their situation.

"Lenny," Silas said, his voice soft, "I understand your fear. We're all scared. But we're also strong, and we're in this together. You made a mistake, a terrible mistake, but I believe in redemption."

Lenny's eyes widened, tears welling up. "You... you forgive me?"

Silas placed a hand on Lenny's shoulder, his eyes filled with compassion. "I do. But you'll have to earn back our trust. Will you help us make things right?"

Lenny nodded, gratitude and determination etched on his face.

The weeks that followed were filled with hard work, forgiveness, and healing. Lenny's redemption was a slow process, but his dedication to making amends was evident.

Dr. Elaine's wit and wisdom were a constant source of comfort, her ability to find humor in the darkest of times a balm for their wounded trust.

"Ah, betrayal," she'd muse, her eyes twinkling. "A spice that can either ruin the dish or add depth to the flavor. It's all in how you cook it."

Silas found himself reflecting on the journey, the highs and lows, the triumphs and failures. He realized that the path to success was not just about innovation and ambition but about empathy, understanding, and the courage to forgive.

As OakLine's resurgence continued, fueled by their AI-driven solution and a renewed sense of purpose, Silas knew that they had not only overcome a great obstacle but had grown stronger in the process.

They had faced betrayal and found redemption. They had looked into the abyss and found their humanity.

And in the quiet moments, when Silas looked out the window at the city that never slept, he knew that OakLine's story was not just about floors or algorithms but about people, dreams, and the indomitable spirit of hope.

Chapter 5: The Turning Point

The OakLine lab had become a crucible of creativity, innovation, and relentless pursuit of excellence. Engineers, designers, programmers, and artisans were working in unison, their minds and hands driven by a shared vision of revolutionizing the flooring industry.

At the heart of it all was the AI-driven solution that Silas and Dr. Elaine had conceived. But this was no ordinary algorithm; it was a symphony of code, design, materials, and artistry. It was a fusion of technology and human creativity that transcended conventional boundaries.

Silas, once the beleaguered CEO, now stood as a conductor orchestrating this technological masterpiece. His eyes sparkled with the passion of a creator, his mind buzzing with ideas that were both profound and audacious.

He walked through the lab, his gaze taking in the various stations where innovation was unfolding:

- **Material Science Station:** Here, AI algorithms were analyzing the molecular structure of different materials, optimizing them for strength, sustainability, and aesthetic appeal. Nanotechnology was being employed to create self-healing surfaces, while biodegradable compounds were ensuring environmental sustainability.

- **Design Hub:** Virtual reality interfaces allowed designers to create and visualize flooring patterns in real-time, guided by AI suggestions based on global design trends, cultural influences, and even individual user preferences. The blend of human intuition and machine precision was creating designs that were breathtakingly beautiful and unique.

- **Production Line:** AI-driven robotic arms were working seamlessly with human craftsmen, cutting, shaping, and assembling the flooring with unprecedented accuracy. Machine learning models were continually refining the production process, reducing waste, and enhancing quality.

- **Quality Control Center:** Advanced sensors and computer

vision algorithms were inspecting every inch of the finished product, ensuring that it met the highest standards of quality. Any imperfection, no matter how minute, was detected and corrected.

Silas's heart swelled with pride as he watched his team, each member a maestro in their field, working in harmony with technology that was as elegant as it was powerful.

Dr. Elaine, ever the whimsical genius, was at her workstation, her fingers dancing across multiple keyboards, her screens filled with complex code and colorful visualizations.

"Ah, Silas," she exclaimed, looking up with a mischievous grin. "I've just taught our AI to appreciate Impressionist art. It's now creating flooring patterns inspired by Monet. Fancy a walk in a virtual garden?"

Silas chuckled, his mind whirling with the possibilities. "Only you, Dr. Elaine, could make floors that evoke the soul of Van Gogh or the serenity of a Zen garden."

They were on the brink of something extraordinary, a product that was not just a surface to walk on but an experience, a statement, a reflection of identity.

But time was against them. The financial pressures were mounting, and Graham's shadow still loomed large. The race was not yet won, and the final stretch was fraught with uncertainty.

Silas knew that they had to bring their creation to market, to prove that OakLine was not just surviving but thriving, leading the way in a new era of design and technology.

As he stood in the lab, surrounded by the hum of innovation, the glow of screens, and the energy of a team that had become a family, Silas made a vow.

They would succeed. They would change the world, one floor at a time.

For OakLine, for innovation, for the dreamers and the creators, the turning point had arrived. The future was now.

Chapter 6: The Deal and The Duel

OakLine's resurgence was nothing short of miraculous. The company's revolutionary AI-driven flooring designs were the talk of the industry, and investors were taking notice. Major clients were lining up, intrigued by the fusion of art, technology, and sustainability that OakLine had achieved.

But success had also drawn the attention of enemies. CedarCorp, once dismissive of OakLine, now saw them as a threat. Graham, CedarCorp's executive, was seething with rage and envy. He had underestimated Silas, underestimated OakLine, and he was determined to rectify his mistake.

In a dimly lit boardroom, Graham assembled his team of corporate warriors, mercenaries who specialized in subterfuge, sabotage, and manipulation.

"Gentlemen," Graham sneered, his eyes cold and calculating, "OakLine has become a problem, and I intend to solve it. By any means necessary."

His plan was as ruthless as it was cunning:

- **Industrial Espionage:** Graham hired hackers to infiltrate OakLine's systems, stealing trade secrets, disrupting their production line, and sowing chaos.

- **Media Manipulation:** Fake news stories were planted, questioning OakLine's ethics, sustainability claims, and even Silas's integrity. A smear campaign designed to tarnish OakLine's reputation and shake investor confidence.

- **Legal Warfare:** Frivolous lawsuits were filed, accusing OakLine of patent infringement, labor violations, and more. The intention was not to win in court but to drain OakLine's resources and distract them from their core business.

- **Hostile Takeover:** CedarCorp began buying up OakLine's shares, attempting a hostile takeover that would give them control of OakLine's innovations without having to pay for them.

Silas was not oblivious to Graham's machinations. He knew that CedarCorp was playing dirty, and he was prepared to fight back.

But the battle was taking its toll, not just on OakLine's finances but on Silas's soul.

In the midst of the corporate war, a potential deal emerged that could change the game. A major client, a global retail giant, was interested in an exclusive partnership with OakLine. The deal was worth millions, but it came with strings attached, demands that challenged OakLine's values and ethics.

Silas found himself in a moral quandary, torn between securing OakLine's future and compromising their integrity. The boardroom became a battleground of ideals, with Silas, Mary, Dr. Elaine, and Jackson wrestling with the decision.

The debates were passionate, the stakes immense, the choices agonizing.

"Silas, we need this deal," Mary argued, her voice filled with desperation. "It's our chance to beat CedarCorp and secure our future."

"But at what cost, Mary?" Silas countered, his eyes filled with torment. "Do we sacrifice our principles, our very soul, to win?"

The tension was palpable, the room charged with emotion, conviction, and fear.

In the end, Silas made the decision to accept the deal, but with conditions that preserved OakLine's integrity. It was a gamble, a high-stakes play that could either catapult OakLine to greatness or send them spiraling into oblivion.

The deal was signed, the celebration bittersweet. OakLine had won a significant battle, but the war with CedarCorp was far from over.

As Silas looked out the window, the city's skyline reflecting his own tumultuous emotions, he knew that the fight had only just begun. The battle for OakLine's soul, for the future of innovation, for the very essence of business ethics, was a fight that he was willing to wage.

For OakLine, for his team, for the dream that had become a mission, Silas was ready to face the storm.

The duel had begun, and the giants were locked in a dance that would leave no one unscathed.

Chapter 7: The Triumph and The Twist

The day of reckoning had arrived. OakLine's groundbreaking product launch was the culmination of innovation, determination, and resilience. The industry's most influential players, media, and even the public were gathered to witness what was being hailed as a revolution in flooring design.

The venue was a marvel in itself, with OakLine's AI-driven floors transforming the space into a living canvas, reflecting art, nature, culture, and technology. The floors seemed to breathe, to tell a story, to connect with the very soul of those who walked on them.

Silas stood backstage, a whirlwind of emotions coursing through him. Pride, anticipation, fear, and excitement mingled in a heady mix that left him both elated and humbled.

Dr. Elaine, resplendent in her colorful attire, winked at him. "Ready to change the world, Silas?"

He smiled, his heart swelling with gratitude for her brilliance, her humor, her unwavering faith in him.

"I think we already have," he replied, his voice filled with conviction.

The presentation was a triumph, a showcase of OakLine's genius, a testament to the power of human creativity and technological prowess. The audience was spellbound, the applause thunderous, the accolades effusive.

Silas's speech was not just about floors or technology; it was about dreams, about innovation as a force for good, about the triumph of integrity over deceit.

As he stood on the stage, basking in the glow of success, he knew that OakLine had not just survived; they had thrived. They had defeated CedarCorp's underhanded tactics, they had stayed true to their values, they had emerged victorious.

The celebration that followed was filled with joy, laughter, and a sense of vindication. The team that had become a family reveled in their success, knowing that they had achieved something extraordinary.

But amidst the jubilation, a shadow lurked.

Unknown to Silas, Graham was watching the event from afar, his face contorted with rage and humiliation. CedarCorp's attempts to destroy OakLine had failed, their reputation tarnished, their dominance threatened.

Graham's eyes narrowed, his mind already plotting, scheming, planning his next move. Silas had won the battle, but the war was far from over.

And then, a twist that no one saw coming.

In the midst of the celebration, Silas received a mysterious message on his phone. A cryptic clue, a riddle that hinted at something bigger, something hidden, something that could change everything.

Silas's heart pounded, his mind racing. What was this message? Who had sent it? What did it mean?

As the party continued around him, Silas stood frozen, the weight of the message sinking in. He looked up, his eyes filled with a mix of wonder and trepidation.

The journey was not over. OakLine's triumph was just the beginning. A new adventure awaited, a mystery to unravel, a path unexplored.

The story of Silas and OakLine had taken a turn, a twist that promised to be as thrilling as it was enigmatic.

The adventure had only just begun.

About the Author

Phill C. Akinwale, PMP has managed operational endeavors, projects and project controls across government and private sectors in various companies, including Motorola, Honeywell, Emerson, Skillsoft, Citigroup, Iron Mountain, Brown and Caldwell, US Airways and CVS Caremark. With his extensive experience in various facets of Project Management and rigorous project controls, he has trained project management worldwide (NASA, FBI, USAF, USACE, US Army, Department of Transport) across five PMBOK® Guide editions over the last 15 years.

He holds twelve project management certifications with six in Agile Project Management (CSM, PMI-ACP, PSM, PSPO, PAL, SPS). As a John Maxwell Certified Coach and Speaker, Phill delivers workshops, seminars, keynote speaking, and coaching in leadership and soft skills. Working together with you and your team or organization, he will guide you in the desired direction and equip you to reach your goals. Books he has authored include: The No-Good Leader, Earned Value Basics and Project Management Mid-Level to C-Level.